Numb to this single life

A collection of poems for all of the single folks

By: Antionette Barnes

Copyright © 2023 Antionette Barnes All rights reserved

The characters and events portrayed in this book are fictitious. Any similarity to real persons, living or dead, is coincidental and not intended by the author.

No part of this book may be reproduced or stored in a retrieval system or transmitte in any form or by any means, electronic, mechanical, photocopying, recording, or otherwise, without express written permission of the publisher.

ISBN-13: 978-1-7370589-1-5

Table of contents:

1. Numb
2. Single
3. Life
4. Time
5. Suffocate
6. Clingy
7. When I wanted you
8. I found myself
9. Loving me for me
10. I've been single for far too long
11. Season
12. Falling in love
13. Falling out of love with
14. You
15. Cry
16. Done being hurt
17. Love too hard
18. Happy lone woman
19. Unstable
20. Forever
21. Mines
22. This single life
23. Looking for love
24. Love in the wrong places
25. Knowing your self-worth
26. When your phone is dry
27. Dry
28. For me
29. Remember you
30. Dating for fun
31. Fall in love with me
32. Mutual
33. Sleeping by myself
34. The effects of cuddling
35. Emotions
36. That one phone call
37. I almost accepted it

38. I felt ugly
39. Head all over the place
40. When I get in my mood
41. Ignored phone calls
42. I see your texts
43. I saw your calls
44. Hit me up
45. Calm
46. Happy
47. Future children
48. To my future self
49. A letter to my old self
50. Have you ever met somebody who have a way with words?
51. Think of
52. Between us
53. I almost gave up
54. Lost hope
55. Comes to mind
56. Playing games
57. Motivated
58. Isolated
59. Confide in you
60. Maybe
61. Deep feeling
62. Deep talk
63. What happened when we first met?
64. Make it make sense
65. Lost interest in me
66. Conversations
67. Questions
68. Kept a secret
69. Talk facts
70. Willing
71. Confided in me
72. Make time
73. You stopped texting me
74. Not going to wait for you
75. Get my time back
76. Mean the most to me
77. You've been blocked

78. Tried to get me back
79. A lifestyle
80. Develop a love for myself

Numb

I grew numb to this lifestyle

See, I've been single for far too long

My hopes of getting out of this lifestyle is dead it seems

I only know this single season

Numb

I've been all alone in my season of being single

Numb

I'm nowhere close to coming out

Intimacy

What is that?

I have not seen an act of true love

Within my season of being single

Single

Single

Is that a season?

For I have been single for far too long

It doesn't seem like it's coming to an end

Single

Is that a calling?

It seems like I'm meant to be single

Am I meant to focus on myself?

Single

What do single people do?

How do single people live?

What does it actually mean to be single?

Life

Life
What is it about this thing call life?
I still haven't quite figure it out yet
Life gets to me a lot

I'm still going through life alone
I still don't have anybody to talk to
Deep conversations are what I be longing for
Deep, deep conversations

Most of the time I can be full of life
Then other times I can be feeling down
What is it about this thing call life?
Life

Time

Time is something we can't get back
Time is something that single people have
Time to be alone
Time to self-reflect

Time is precious
So, wisely is how it should be used
Use your time to plan your future
For a better future should be a goal

With nothing but time on your hand
There shouldn't be any excuses as to what you can't do
Time is ticking
Don't let time past you by

Suffocate

**She is lying in bed
As quiet as can be
Trying her hardest
Not to suffocate**

**Breathing
She is starting to breath hard
Gasping
Struggling for air**

**She is missing him like crazy
How can she go on without him?
She don't know what to do
Suffocate**

**Inhale, exhale
Take deep breathes and breath
Revive
Life goes on**

Clingy

See, I used to be the clingy type
Always wanting to be up under him
Never wanted to be alone
I just had to be with him

Don't leave me
Stay with me
Clingy
I don't want to be separated from you

I was losing myself
Not valuing my alone time
Scared to be alone, was I?
I just had to be in his arms

When I wanted you

I was loyal
I dropped all of them for you
I was all about you
You, you

I just wanted you
Your opinions matter the most to me
I wouldn't go nowhere if you told me not to
But that was when I wanted you

I wanted you....
I wanted you so bad
That I would do almost anything for you
But now that has all changed.

I found myself

**Lost in this world
No hand to hold
Walking by myself
Am I on the right path?**

**Struggling to find my way
Don't know who I really am
Trying to find myself
Where do I start?**

**Questioning myself
Speaking life to myself
Well, I can finally say that
"I found myself"**

Loving me for me

The news has finally come out
My eyes has finally open to a new me
I am now seeing myself in a whole new light
It's time to put myself first

Loving me for me
Yeah, that sounds good
Loving me for me
I should have been did that

A long time ago,
I should had been had confidence in myself
Loving me for me
Loving me for who I truly am

I've been single for far too long

Where do I start?
My love life?
Hmm
I've been single for far too long

Long, meaningful kisses
Two arms wrapped around me
Warm cuddling
Are these forms of intimacy?

Deep conversations with that special person
Is what I long for
I've been single for far too long
Can't you tell?

Season

Going through this season alone
And I do mean, I'm rocking solo
I have no one to call my own
I've been single for far too long

Is it true that "being single" is a season?
Because I've been in this season of being single for many years
At times, it seems like my season of being single has been expired
But yet I'm still single

This season of singleness is not for everybody
Is it?
This so-called season of singleness, I'm ready to get out of it
My season of being single has expired

Or is the expiration date coming soon?
For I am ready to be with my soulmate
Be united with them at last
From season of singleness to being with my lifelong partner

Falling in love

Falling in love is easy
No!
Falling in love is hard
Maybe!

Being single will have you learning your worth
Falling in love with anybody is not for me
I value me

How can I fall in love with that special someone?
I have been single for a very long time
Falling in love sounds so good
Falling in love sounds so easy

I want love
I want my special someone
Falling in love with love
Forever

Falling out of love with love

Falling out of love with love is not easy
Who would want to fall out of love when they are so in love?
Letting go of someone who you love dearly is not easy
Their type of love might be the only type of love that they know and lo

Falling out of love with love
That sounds so bad
Falling in love with love
Yeah, that sounds good

You

I was once single
Going through life the best way I saw fit
Then the day came
When I met you

You were not like the others
There was something about you in the beginning
Every time I looked at you
I tried and tried to figure it out

What was it about you that had me drawn to you?
I used to go throughout my days thinking about you
Until the thought finally hit me
You were everything that I prayed for plus more

Cry

This was something that I did a lot
I barely knew why I did it
I just know that I did
It was something that I wanted to change

It just had to change
Something had to give
Tears flowing down my face
I just couldn't do it no more

Every small thing you did to me,
Made tears fall down my face
I just had to release my grasp that I had on you
So, that my "cry" of hurt would stop

It stopped
The tears stopped flowing
My "cry" of hurt stopped
That's when "peace" came

Done being hurt

I've been hurt so many times
Hurt by people I love
Hurt by people I thought couldn't do no wrong to me
I was hurt until I couldn't be hurt anymore

What's going on here?
I can't take it no more
It has to stop
I'm done being hurt
Opening up easy is not an option

Done being hurt
Yes, I am
I love too hard to allow myself to be hurt
My hurt changed me

Love too hard

I used to put my all into relationships
Trying to get closer to certain individuals
I just had to let them know my worth
Why didn't they see my worth?

I had my priorities all messed up
Putting people first
Who put me last
Why didn't I see things clearly before?

I used to love too hard
Loving too hard constantly brought tears to my eyes
I was down a lot
Stress out on what I could have been changed

Why did I always used to love too hard?
Lessons were made from the mistakes
The mistakes of loving too hard
Putting myself first has became a top priority of mines

The happy lone woman

You looked at her
And thought she was miserable
Just because she was a lone woman
Not knowing that she was a happy lone woman

Her freedom meant way more to her
Than being in a "no good" relationship
That lone woman
Was a happy lone woman

She was the type
Who wasn't the easy type
She pushed people away
Even if it meant that she would continue on being a lone woman

Unstable

How could you expect somebody to fall in love with you?
You didn't even love yourself
You were broken inside
That brokenness showed

You were unstable
An unstable being
You were unable to express your love
Is it safe to say that you didn't know how?

You can't tell me that you weren't unstable
I knew first hand
Remember when your emotions
Kept going out of control

Unstable!
Remember those times I tried to get you to communicate your feelings to me?
Is it safe to say that you were at war with yourself?
Love yourself first

Forever

You was my forever
I wanted to spend the rest of my life with you
I wanted nobody but you
You couldn't see that

Why couldn't you see that?
The signs were all there
Right in front of you
I even told your ears

Forever
You and I
Reality
I had to face reality

You seen the signs
You knew what was up
You just didn't want me
You wasted my time

Mines

I wish I knew how
To make you interested in me
Then I would know how to make you mines
Forever mines

If only there was a way
Then I would be wrapped up in your arms
Feeling the love from your arms
If only there were some signs

On how to make you mines
Then I would be happy in love
I will make you mines
That's a fact for sure

This single life

This single life is easy
This single life is enjoyable
This single life is peaceful
Don't let nobody tell you otherwise

With this single life
Comes transformation
Empowering oneself
Enjoying alone time

Embrace your singleness
Walk the path of your trip
Your trip of finding your true self
This single life is for you

Looking for love

I've been looking and looking
With what seems to be in vain
No signs no where
Not here or far

At times, I be wanting to give up
It doesn't seem like I am close
Looking for love
I'm close to giving up

Am I looking for love
In the wrong places?
Love don't seem to want to find me
What am I to do when love won't find me?

My heart be calling out
Calling out for love
I've been looking for love
For what seems to be an eternity

Love in the wrong places

I used to search and search
Trying to find me some love
Traveling down the wrong paths
Love in the wrong places

Getting hurt
Time and time again
Left behind
Getting picked over for others

Self-esteem was low
Couldn't get confidence in myself
Trying to find love in all the wrong places
Crying myself to sleep

Pillows wet
Sleep lost
Self lost
All become I didn't learn to love myself first

Knowing your self-worth

Knowing your self-worth
Will have you single
Knowing your self-worth
Will have you at peace with yourself

Being single for a long period of time
Will have you learning yourself all over again
Loving your true self
Is apart of knowing your self-worth

Valuing one's self
Boosting up one's self-confidence
Standing firm on their "No"
Are all apart of knowing one's self-worth

When your phone is dry

Sitting here thinking
All in my thoughts
What am I to do
When I feel so alone?

What can you do
When your phone is dry?
There is no one to talk to
At least that's what it seems

When your phone is dry
It can make you feel unloved
Am I on anyone's brain?
Am I running through anyone's head?

Dry

Conversations with you
Are just not the same anymore
Your texts started to get short
Your tone with me changed

I sensed it
Way before you went "dry"
Something in me told me
It warned me

Something told me that you weren't the one
Way before you went "dry"
But I just didn't want to see it
I didn't want it to be true

You changed up on me
You stopped fooling with me
Used to hit me up everyday
All of a sudden, you went "dry"

For me

I don't have to worry about anything anymore
What's for me
Is for me
I used to always search for who is for me

I had to learn that the long way
Yeah
For me
I used to always search for who is for me

Not knowing that I needed to let it be
Leave it alone
Because if it's for me
I would know

Who is for me
Is for me
Just let it be natural
I had to learn that on my own

Remember you

I remember that time
When I was down and out
I had no one to talk to
Nowhere to turn to

I started talking to God
Started talking to myself
Then you came along
That's when all that changed

I remember you
I remember us
You gave me words of encouragement
You didn't even know it

I remember you
You were one of the realist ones
Always positive vibes
When you came around

Dating for fun

**It's been a good hot minute
Since I've been in love
To the point
That I don't know how love feels anymore**

**Loving hard is what I do
I give my all to the one who I believe is for me
So, when dating comes into mind
I don't date for fun**

**No, I don't date for fun
I don't play around
I speak my mind
Speak my truth**

**My heart is guarded
It's hard to get through
Dating for fun
Is so not for me**

Fall in love with me
It might take you awhile
But you will get there
You will realize
That I'm the one for you

Then at that point
You'll fall in love with me
Truly fall in love with me
But don't let it be too late

Because at some point
If it's too late
I will fall out of love with you
Because I'm not in the waiting around business

Mutual

These feelings are mutual
Well, I wish they were mutual
Loving you
Thinking about you

Day in/ Day out
Mutual
But you're so far away
You've been so distant

Spilling my heart out to you
I used to spill my heart out to you
Wanting you to feel how I was feeling
Wishing these feelings were mutual

Sleeping by myself

This is something that I'm used to
At night by myself
Curled up
Hugging my pillows

There's an empty spot on the side of me
No one is really ever there
Sleeping by myself
I've learned to look forward to it

I embrace my loneliness
Sleeping by myself
Waking up alone
To the quietness of my room

I be wanting to cuddle
At the same time
I love to be alone
I be sleeping alone

The effects of cuddling

Cuddling feels so good
When it's done with the right one
Cuddling feels so good
When it hasn't been done to you in awhile

The connection
The vibe
The energy
Are real when they are with the right person

Intimacy on a whole different level
Comfort
Security
These are all effects of cuddling

Emotions

Lately, I've been dealing with different emotions
All at war with each other
Within me
I don't know how long I can keep them in

They're all screaming to get out
Fighting to get out
They're at war inside of me
Keeping them in is hurting me

I have to let them all out
These emotions got me confused
How am I suppose to feel?
There're too many emotions

They're all woke
I just want to be at peace
I'm confused on how to feel
These emotions are at war

That one phone call

Hmm,
That one phone call
Yes, I want it
I'm expecting it

Call me, call me, call me
That one phone call
That one phone call
From my special somebody

Got me waiting by the phone
Got me keeping my line open
I'm numb to this single life
That don't mean I don't be expecting that one phone call

I almost accepted it

I must admit
I was once a fool
Allowing people to treat me any kind of way
I accepted it

I had to put an end to it
I got tired of it
Then I met you
You did stuff that I almost accepted

You used to hit me up
When it was convenient to you
I started to feel like I was convenience to you
I almost accepted it

I felt ugly

**I felt ugly
When I didn't get looked at
I felt ugly
When I didn't get a text**

**I felt ugly
Around people
I felt ugly
Everyday**

**I felt ugly
When I didn't get a FaceTime call
I felt ugly
When I looked in the mirror**

**I felt ugly,
I felt ugly,
I felt ugly,
My self-esteem was crushed**

Head all over the place

One minute, I'm thinking about this
The next minute, I'm thinking about that
My head is all over the place
I can't think straight

I want to be in a relationship
I want to be single
I want love but
I love my peace

My head is all over the place
I'm numb to this single life
But I don't want to be single
Soulmate me please

I love my independency
At the same time, I want a dominant partner
Submissive!
What is that?

When I get in my mood

When I get in my mood,
I don't want to be bothered
Small things irate me
Normal things frustrate me

I don't want to be bothered
I just want to be left alone
Please stop talking to me
Just go away

When I get in my mood
I shut myself from the world
Social outcast, am I?
I just be wanting to be to my lonely

Ignored phone calls

This is nothing new
I'm used to it
In other words,
I'm numb to it

I called and called
No response
No call back
Are you busy?

It seemed to be a habit
I caught on to the signs
No communication
Is that you telling me you don't want to talk to me?

My calls decreased in number
My communication ceased
Moving on is the best option
Ring....Is that you calling?

I see your texts

**Sitting here
Doing nothing
Sitting here
With my phone in my hand**

**When I noticed a notification
It was a message from you
Why are you texting me?
Ignored**

**I don't fool with you
I see your texts
Phone goes off with some more notifications
Some more texts from you**

**I'm over you
I moved on from you
Can't you see?
Ignored**

I saw your calls

You thought you had me
When you called,
I used to answer all the time
First ring was it?

Second ring maybe?
I used to call back when I couldn't answer
I put you as a priority
Until I noticed

I used to get ignored a lot by you
It would be a whole new day or days
When you would respond to me
I caught on quick

I stopped hitting you up
You noticed
You started blowing me up a lot
I ignored you

I saw your calls
I have you to know
I watched as you called me
I read your texts

I saw your calls
I have you to know that you are no longer a priority to me
Sad to say
I almost fell for you....Hard

Hit me up

I used to always wanted you to hit me up
I got upset when you didn't
I used to always check my phone
Looking for notification from you

Ding...
My phone went off
It wasn't you
Why wasn't you hitting me up?

Then finally,
You did what I wanted you to do
You hit me up with a simple
"Hello ma'am"

Calm

I had to stay calm
Because I was screaming in my head
Screaming real loud
I couldn't let it come out

I had to stay calm
I'm single
Why am I single?
Calm down

Take deep breaths
I have to stay calm
But I can't
I don't want to be single forever

My head is about to explode
With all this screaming
Calm down
Take deep breaths

Happy

I'm happy to say
That I'm finally here at
A point in my life
Where I accept who I am

I'm a single person with flaws
I'm not perfect
I'm who I love
I'm happy

I have self-respect
I value myself
Yes, I'm happy
Happy to say that I'm embracing my "single" self

Future children

To my future children,

I'm sorry

Sorry that it took so long

So long to bring y'all here

Here to meet big brother

You see

Mama have been single for a very long time

Mama wants to make sure that you a great as y'all father

Things are not always easy

Easy as they sound

Big brother wants some siblings

But the way that mama's life has been set up....

To my future self

Girl, you got this
Hold on a little longer
You are not your past
Keep moving forward

Do it bigger and bigger each time
Continue on motivating yourself
Remember how your "old" self used to be?
Your past self?

Keep reminding yourself
That you have to be better than your "old" self
To my future self,
"I love you"

A letter to my old self

I had to write this
I had to get things off my chest
I came along way from who I used to be
This is a letter to my old self

You made a lot of mistakes
That you might or might not regret
You crossed a lot of paths
Of people who taught you lessons

Lessons on life and lessons about people
It took you awhile
Awhile to wise up
When you did wise up, you saw the world so much clearer

Have you ever met somebody who has a way with words?

**Have you ever met somebody
Who has a way with words?
I mean whatever they said,
You believed it?**

**Even if something tells you
That they are lying
Have you ever met somebody
Who has a way with words?**

**A sweet talker?
A persuasive tone of voice?
A talkative person?
Well, I say to stay away from them**

Think of

**Think of all of the things you can do alone
By yourself
In your own solidarity world
Think of everything**

**Limitless possibilities
Do things on your own time
Do things for you
And I do mean for you**

**Spend some time alone
Think of what you want to do
See how you can do it
Go do it**

Between us

Floating
Floating
I can't come down
You swept me off my feet

This is not just between us
Everybody knows
Between us
There is nobody

What have you done to me?
I will love you forever and ever
You can count on that
And this is not just between us

I almost gave up

So, we all know
That I've been single for awhile
It had started taking a toll on me
I almost gave up

At first there were nobody talking to me
As if they weren't interested in me
Phone not going off
I always wondered if anybody was thinking about me

Then you came along
You changed things up for me
You changed my way of thinking
Just when I almost gave up

Lost hope

Lost hope
I almost failed
Lost hope
What am I to do?

Lost hope
My faith was almost gone
Lost hope
I started losing myself

Lost hope
I started going into a dark place
Found myself
I found new hope

Comes to mind

What comes to mind when you think of me?
Be honest
You can tell me the truth
Do you really like me?

What comes to mind when you see me?
Am I the type of female you want?
These are the things I want to know
I have to know

What comes to mind when you hear my voice?
Do I have the type of voice that you can listen to all the time?
Am I your type?
Tell me what comes to mind

Playing games

People be asking
Why am I single?
Do I have a boyfriend?
So, I give them my answers

I normally be like,
"It's in God's hands"
Now, I'm like
"I'm single because I don't be playing games

When I love,
I love hard
And that's for sure
I'm not about playing games

I will speak my mind
I will tell it how I feel
If I want you, I want you and if I don't then I just don't
Because I'm not about playing games

Motivated

Whoa!
It took me awhile
And I do mean a good hot minute
For me to finally come to this place in my life

For me to really want to change
I had to get focus on becoming a better me
Be motivated

Stay motivated
Found out what I really want
Discover my true self
I'm on a path to self-recovery

Isolated

I was so isolated
Cast away from the world
For a lengthy period of time
Doubtful if anymore missed me

I was kept away for far too long
So, when isolation left
I didn't know how to approach the world
So, I didn't know how to react when you approached me

Don't get me wrong
I really like you
I think
I'm not sure

You have to understand
That I've been in isolation for a lengthy period of time
Bare with me
I will get thing called "communication" together eventually

Confide in you

I wish I can confide in you
Tell you all of the things that's been on my mind lately
But you are not mine
You belong to someone else

You make me feel so comfortable
You make me come out of my shell
I'm not shy around you
You have that effect on me

I can't confide in you
I don't know what you'll do with my thoughts and feelings
You belong to someone else
Who am I to confide in now?

Maybe

Maybe I'm meant to be single
Maybe I'm not
Who knows?
Because I don't

Maybe I missed my opportunities of love
Maybe they will come back
Maybe they won't
This is something to wonder

I reflect on some of the times that I might was closed to being in love
Then a light bulb went off in my head
They were just test runs
Maybe I'm meant to be single

Deep feeling

I had this deep feeling that you were not the one
But I kept talking to you
Anyway
Even though I had that deep feeling

I just knew
But I didn't want to know
What I did wanted to know
Was that you were mines

Or that you were almost mines
I just wanted you to be mines
But you hurt me
You hurt me so bad when you called me "friend"

Deep talk

I never really had those kinds of talks
You know
The kinds where you sit for a long period of time
I'm past due for a deep talk

I never really had anyone to talk to
A deep talk here and there would be nice
I never had anyone to tell my dreams to
I was always alone

At least that's how I felt
I never really had anyone to talk about life
About men
About....I'm long overdue for a deep talk

What happened when we first met?

It was a day that I can't forget
It was a day that I was losing hope
I was giving up
I thought I was going to be single forever

Then the day came
When I met you
We didn't meet in person on that day
Don't you remember when first met?

What happened when we first met?
You inbox me with "looking eyes"
When I responded,
Our conversation grew

Instant connection
Sparks flying
Butterflies fluttering
Don't you remember what happened when we first met?

Make it make sense

You told me you didn't want her no more
You told me you were leaving her
You told me you wanted to be with me forever
You called me your "wife"

That was a while ago
I still see her posting y'all together
Make it make sense
You told me you weren't leading me on

Your actions say other wise
No phone conversation when you are around her
My time cut short when she calls you
Make it make sense

Lost interest in me

Yeah, I knew it
I just didn't want to believe it
I didn't want to be alone
You were my companion

You lost interest in me
Way before I knew it
You hid it from me
You hid it well

You were physically there with me
But you weren't mentally there with me
All the time
If only I knew your heart was somewhere else

Conversations

What is it about these conversations of ours?
What is it about them that got me so hooked on you?
I usually prefer calls over texts
For the most part

But your sweet texts
I be looking forward to them
These conversations of ours
Started off short

But now they have extended
How can one fall in love through texts?
Because I think I'm falling in love with you
These conversations of ours are conversations of therapy

Questions

You always do that
Get mad when I ask you questions
Questions that you don't want to answer
Questions about you

Questions about us
Well, I have some questions
Why do you want to be in my life?
Where do you see us years from now?

These are questions
That requires answers of certainty
Are you willing to be with me for a long time
Or just a short time?

Kept a secret

I wasn't the one who you went out
We don't ever be seen in public together
We always kept a low profile
Why is that?

Your house
How do the inside of that looks?
Friends and family
I can't even name one of them

Always in private
We are always meeting up in private
I guess that was how you wanted it
Turns out, I was kept a secret

Talk facts

You are going to hear what I have to say
If you want to be with me
I have some words to share with you
They are nothing but facts

You know that I talk facts
What is wrong with me telling you how I feel?
I talk facts
So, I will tell you how you make me feel

What are relationships about
If we can't talk facts with each other?
No communication means no relationship
Because what are we doing?

Willing

I'm more than willing
To change my relationship status
I'm willing
Do you hear me?

You must believe me
But I'm so numb
I'm numb to this single life
Being single is what I know

There will have to be a lot of effort
For me to be with you
Even though I'm numb to this single life,
I'm still willing to give up this life style

Confided in me

You confided in me
It seemed so easy
We were cool
But I didn't know we were cool like that

Your words fell on trusting ears
You can be sure that these lips
Are lips of honesty
I won't utter a word to a soul

That is unless you want me to
You confided in me
You told me what was heavy on your mind
These trusting ears took in every word

Make time

I found that used to always make time for you
Even when you barely made time for you
Used to claim that you were always busy
Too busy for me

I used to make time
That was how I showed you
That I wanted you
Well, that was one way

All of that has changed
You wonder why I don't make time for you no more
Busy making time for "me"
I make time for who I want to make time for

You stopped texting me

So, you think that I care?
You think that I care that you stopped texting?
We barely used to text
So, why should I care?

You stopped texting me
That was an invitation for me to stop texting you
Letting go was easy
I had no attachment to you

Not going to wait for you

One thing I know how to do is be alone
Another thing to know how to do is move on
Wait for who?
I'm not going to wait for you

Who do you play me for?
If you can't realize
That I'm the one for you by now
Then there is no reason for me to stick around

I'm not going to wait for you
Not an option
I move on quick
I rather be alone

Get my time back

There is no way I can get my time back
My time that was wasted
When you were in my life
Taking up life

There is no way I can get my time back
When time has already passed
Passed by so quickly
Without me even seeing it

There is no way that I can get my time back
That precious time of mine
On the other hand, there is way
That I can make the best of the time that I have now

Mean the most to me

**You were starting to mean the most to me
In my love life
Key word "starting"
That all changed**

**When you started treating me different
You allowed me to see a different side of you
That was a side
That pushed me away from you**

**Just when you starting to mean the most to me
I quickly existed your life
That changing up
Tore us apart**

You've been blocked

On so many occasion
You've been blocked
Blocked on everything
Blocked out of my life

I just wanted to get rid of you
I wanted to erase you out of my mind
Plan failed
You've been blocked

Not erased from my mind
You're still there
Lurking around
Just won't leave

Tried to get me back

When you had me,
You didn't take me seriously
Not caring about my feelings
Not wanting to hear my thoughts

I gave you signs that I was going to leave you
You didn't pick up the signs
I finally left you
All of a sudden

Your act got together
You tried to get me back
But I was too far gone
Now I'm moving on my own

A calling

A calling
A season
A status
No, this is a lifestyle

Wake up single
Go to sleep single
Living life single
This is a lifestyle

It is a lifestyle worth living
Freedom, freedom
Heart full of single ways
This is a lifestyle

Develop a love for myself

I used to torture myself
Straight up talked down on myself
I didn't really love myself
Negative thoughts

Flooded my head
I didn't develop a love for myself
I wasn't with all of that
Compared myself to others

I really talked down on myself
Low self-esteem
No confidence in myself
I had to look at myself in the mirror

Tell myself "You are beautiful"
Spoke life to myself
I had to develop a love for myself
I was sinking quick

Straight into depression
I have to get this off my chest
Depression is not a cool place to be in
I had to get out of that place quick

I have to develop love for myself
Truly love myself
Put myself first
Won't nobody love me the way I love me

Books by this author:
Poetry From The Heart

Unlock What's Deep Inside: An affirmation journal

Leave me to my thoughts

www.ingramcontent.com/pod-product-compliance
Lightning Source LLC
Chambersburg PA
CBHW071026080526
44587CB00015B/2513